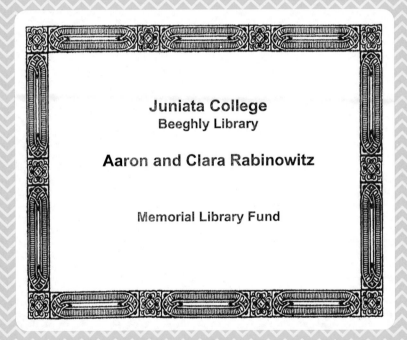

THE LITTLE BOOK OF LITTLE ACTIVISTS

with an introduction by Bob Bland,
co-chair of the Women's March on Washington

&

afterword by Lynda Blackmon Lowery,
author of *Turning 15 on the Road to Freedom*

VIKING

INTRODUCTION

On January 21, 2017, millions of people marched all over the world, in more than five hundred cities across the United States and on all seven continents. They were marching in support of women's rights, civil liberties, and equality. They were marching to show that their opinions mattered and their voices could not be ignored. The Women's March was the largest mass mobilization in United States history, and I helped make it happen.

I wasn't a professional political organizer, and I'd never done anything like this before. It all just started with an idea. I thought that women should march on Washington, DC, and stand together against racism, sexism, and xenophobia. I believed that we could make the government hear us. So I started a Facebook event for a march. In a matter of hours, this idea became a movement.

What many people didn't know was that I was nine months pregnant with my second child at that time. When we began to work collectively on giving life to the March, I was already deep in preparation for bringing a new life into this world. I gave birth to my daughter, Chloe, just six weeks before we marched.

Chloe was lucky to be welcomed into an environment of love and peace. Many children are not as fortunate and are not able to exercise the right to protest, to sit high on parents' shoulders and carry signs of resistance in the streets. This book is a celebration of that right. I stand in gratitude with parents who teach their children to push back in the face of oppression and prejudice and to use their voices, no matter how little, to speak up for marginalized communities.

It is a feat to teach children about racial and social justice without robbing them of their innocence. For those parents who embrace this challenge and seek to lead lives of activism for themselves and their children, this book is for you. For the kids who stand up against bullying, whether it be in their schools, communities, home lives, or government, this book is for you.

The Women's March on Washington signified a new wave of activism for many, and a new chapter in my life, too. People from all walks of life joined together in solidarity, many of them engaging in social activism for the first time. This book seeks to inspire them and others to keep on resisting. And to remind us all that the future is in the hands of our children, and they are poised and ready for action.

—Bob Bland,
co-chair of the Women's March on Washington

ACTIVISM

Taking action in order to create social change.

Anyone can be an activist.

"We need to make our generation a nicer one. **If there's a mess, it's our job to fix it.**"

—Carsyn, age 11

—Loïe, age 2

—Xaviana, age 5½

"I read about other marches and I saw other kids marching to tell the bullies they were WRONG. I thought: I could do that, too."

—Xaviana, age 5½

"If you want to
make a change
in the world,
go ahead.

–Lucy, age 8, Penny, age 7, & Sophia

Nobody can stop you."

–Eden, age 9

—Jayna, age 9

FEMINISM

The belief that **women and men deserve equal rights**, opportunities, and respect.

"Feminism means that **women** get to make their own decisions and **can do anything they strive for.**"

—Cailyn, age 6

"**Kids can do anything** they set their minds to! You just have to

keep speaking up, keep **moving forward,**

and don't get discouraged if people don't take you seriously at first. Adults are harder to convince than kids."

—Mari, age 9

I AM A GIRL
I AM SMART
I AM STRONG
I CAN DO ANYTHING
Peace On Earth

—Eden, age 9

—Xander, age 6, & Owen, age 8

GIRLS SHOULD BE TREATED FAIRLY

WE WILL NOT BE SILENCED

17 WOMEN'S MARCH

—Alex, age 2

"Be active.

If everyone starts
fighting for what
they believe in,

we could
change
the world."

—Aria, age 9

DEMOCRACY

A government that's run by the people.

The people decide who is in charge by voting in free, fair, and frequent elections.

The leaders have to tell the people what they're doing in government.

If the people don't like what their leaders are doing, then in the next election they can vote for someone else.

No one is guaranteed to be the leader. They only get to be in charge if the people choose them.

—Eleanor & Abigail

NOT IN MY
NEIGHBORHOOD
☮ ⊘HATE⊘ JUST SAY NO!

NO HATE
☮ IN OUR ☮
NEIGHBOR-
⊘ HOOD ☮

I HAVE A DREAM
TO LIVE IN LOVE
AND PEACE

—Malak, age 8

—Birdie, age 18 months

"I care about equality in our country, because I want to

FIGHT for those who don't have A VOICE,

and because I want to choose
the kind of world I will inherit."

—Gabriela, age 13

FIRST AMENDMENT RIGHTS

These are things that every single person in the United States has the right to do, that the government can't punish you for.

☆ Saying what you don't like about your country or its leaders.

☆ Publishing and broadcasting your opinions and information.

☆ Practicing any religion you want, or no religion at all.

☆ Assembling peacefully with a group of people, like for a rally, protest, or march.

☆ Telling the government when you don't like what they're doing, and asking them to change.

—AJ, age 11

RACISM
CRIMINAL JUSTICE REFORM
PLANNED PARENTHOOD
EQUALITY
the future
CLIMATE CHANGE
SCIENCE
FOR HER
WOMEN'S RIGHTS
WHY I MARCH

PLA
IS IN
HOU
AND
SENA

We are the FUTURE and the future is BRIGHT

—Nora, age 3

IMMIGRANTS We Get THE JOB DONE

—Sophie, age 5

PROTEST

Disrupting the usual flow of things in order to **call attention** to an injustice and **demand that it be changed.**

Some types of protests:

☆ Boycotts
☆ Petitions
☆ Demonstrations
☆ Sit-ins
☆ Walkouts
☆ Picketing

ONE WORLD

"Our lives begin to end the day we become silent about things that matter."

- Martin Luther King, Jr

PEACE AND LOVE NOW! ALWAYS!

Peace, love, care, ALWAYS!

IS LOVE, IS LOVE, IS LOVE

—Molly & Bennett

"Kids have a voice!

We can change the world by taking a stand for our future.

We can have shared dialogue and discussion about our ideals, and learn to be respectful even when we hear something we don't agree with."

—Gabriela, age 13

GIRLS
SHOULD BE
TREATED
EQUALLY

—Amali, age 9

"Don't be scared

to **say what you mean** and **share what you believe.**

If you do it **kindly** and **respectfully**, you can get your message across."

—Kennedy, age 11

— JJ

FREEDOM

The power to **do as you see fit with your own body and your own property,** as long as it doesn't hurt anybody else's body or property.

"To be free means to believe what you want to believe, and not to have anyone control you. **You get to make your own decisions.**"

—Carsyn, age 11

—Sophie & Emma, age 5

WHERE THERE IS OPPRESSION THERE IS RESISTANCE

—Lola, age 5

I
MARCHED
before I
Walked

—Leha, age 5 months

EQUALITY

"Equality means
having the
same rights
and being **treated fairly.**
One person is not better
than another person.
WE ARE ALL IMPORTANT
no matter how much money
we have or how pretty we are,
or our gender or race."

—Carsyn, age 11

—Brennan, age 8, & Zuri, age 6

MI PAPA ES
INMIGRANTE
LO AMO

—Stella, age 11

"It makes **zero sense**
to say that people are different
just because their skin is a
different color or they were born
somewhere else.

My sister has **yellow hair**
and I have **brown hair,**

**but we're sisters
and I love her."**

—Xaviana, age 5½

"Speak the truth, even if your voice shakes."

—Maddie, age 14

Future
Leader

—Cora

I started speaking up for civil rights and equality when I was a little girl, back in the 1950s and '60s. My mother died when I was seven years old. She was sick and she didn't get proper medical treatment just because she was black. I heard my grandmother say, "She wouldn't have died if she hadn't been colored."

I made a vow right then: "When I get big, I will change things, so no other child will ever have to grow up without a mother because of the color of her skin."

What I didn't know was that I wouldn't have to wait until I got big.

When I was thirteen, I heard Dr. Martin Luther King, Jr., give a speech to the grown-ups about getting the right to vote. He talked about nonviolence and how you could persuade people to do things your way with "steady, loving confrontation." Those three words shaped my life, and now I want to give them to you. Don't stop when you get tired or discouraged—that's the steady part. Don't give in to hate—that's the loving part. And stand up to the bullying with the power of your people—that's confrontation.

By the time I was fifteen years old, I had been in jail nine times, because I kept protesting the segregation and un-equal rights between black and white people. In 1965 I went to a big voting rights march, where I was the youngest person to walk across Alabama, from my home in Selma to the state capital in Montgomery. I celebrated my fifteenth birthday while I was on the march! Thousands of people, both black and white, participated in that march for equality. And it worked. Five months later, Congress passed the Voting Rights Act of 1965, giving citizens across the USA—women and men, black and white—the right to vote. It was an awesome feeling to know I had been a part of that change.

The Selma Movement was a kids' movement. We didn't know it at the time, but we were making history. You have a voice too, and with determination, you can be a history maker just like me. You are never too young to fight nonviolently for what you believe in. Pick a cause that matters to you and work on it until you effect change. Be determined to carry it through, no matter the outcome. If you believe in yourself and you see something wrong, and you work to make it better, then I truly believe you can change the world.

Remember: history can't happen without you.

—Lynda Blackmon Lowery,
author of *Turning 15 on the Road to Freedom:
My Story of the 1965 Selma Voting Rights March*

VIKING
Penguin Young Readers
An imprint of Penguin Random House LLC
375 Hudson Street
New York, New York 10014

First published in the United States of America by Viking,
an imprint of Penguin Random House LLC, 2017

LIBRARY OF CONGRESS CATALOGING-IN-PUBLICATION DATA IS AVAILABLE
ISBN 9780451478542

Printed in China   Edited by Leila Sales   Design by Mariam Quraishi
Creative consultation by Tabitha St. Bernard-Jacobs

1   3   5   7   9   10   8   6   4   2

A nonprofit founded in 1973, the **Children's Defense Fund** exists to provide a strong,
effective, and independent voice for all the children of America, paying particular
attention to the needs of poor children, children of color, and those with disabilities.
**Five percent of the proceeds from the sale of this book goes to support the
Children's Defense Fund's Freedom Schools® program**, which engages more
than 13,000 children and youths annually with proven empowerment
and reading enrichment programs. CDF Freedom Schools are
developing the next generation of leaders to reweave the fabric
of community for children and youth.

To learn more about the Children's Defense Fund
and CDF Freedom Schools, visit us online at
www.childrensdefense.org/LittleActivists.